HEALING YOUR HOLIDAY GRIEF

Also by Alan Wolfelt:

Creating Meaningful Funeral Ceremonies:
A Guide for Families

Healing a Friend's Grieving Heart:
100 Practical Ideas for Helping Someone
You Love Through Loss

Healing a Teen's Grieving Heart:
100 Practical Ideas for Families, Friends
and Caregivers

Healing Your Grieving Heart for Kids:
100 Practical Ideas

The Journey Through Grief:
Reflections on Healing

Understanding Your Grief:
Ten Essential Touchstones For Finding
Hope and Healing Your Heart

When Your Pet Dies:
A Guide to Mourning, Remembering,
and Healing

*Companion Press is dedicated to the education and
support of both the bereaved and bereavement caregivers.*

*We believe that those who companion the bereaved by
walking with them as they journey in grief have a
wondrous opportunity: to help others embrace and grow
through grief—and to lead fuller, more deeply-lived lives
themselves because of this important ministry.*

Companion

For a complete catalog and
ordering information, write or call:

Companion Press
The Center for Loss and Life Transition
3735 Broken Bow Road
Fort Collins, CO 80526
(970) 226-6050
www.centerforloss.com

HEALING YOUR HOLIDAY GRIEF

100 PRACTICAL IDEAS
FOR BLENDING MOURNING AND CELEBRATION
DURING THE HOLIDAY SEASON

•

ALAN D. WOLFELT, PH.D.

Companion
PRESS

Fort Collins, Colorado
An imprint of the Center for Loss and Life Transition

Companion Press is an imprint of the
Center for Loss and Life Transition,
3735 Broken Bow Road, Fort Collins, Colorado 80526
(970) 226-6050
ww.centerforloss.com

Companion Press books may be purchased in bulk for sales promotions, premiums or fundraisers. Please contact the publisher at the above address for more information.

Printed in the United States of America

15 14 13 12 11   5 4 3 2

ISBN: 978-1-87965-148-7.

To all the grieving families who have shared their holiday stories with me and so lovingly demonstrated how to blend mourning and celebration

INTRODUCTION

If you could go back in time to relive a special holiday, which one would you choose?

Close your eyes for a moment and think about this holiday. Now, slowly, walk through this memory in your mind.

What made it so special? What were the surroundings like? What touch sensations do you recall? What sounds can you remember? What smells laced the air? Are there certain tastes you associate with this particular holiday?

Who inhabits this memory with you? Can you picture him? Can you hear her speak? What are your feelings for this person, for this day?

Holidays have such rich associations for us because humankind created them as a way to honor and celebrate that which is truly important. We step out of the hustle and bustle of our day-to-day routines and into a world where our spiritual beliefs and connection to others matter above all else. We give pause to give thanks, and we share of ourselves.

As the Grinch learned that memorable Christmas, the holidays don't really come from a store—they come from the heart and soul.

Which is why, when someone loved dies, the holidays can be so very painful. The heart of the holidays has been torn apart. Without love, what is life? Without the people we love, what are the holidays?

I want you to know that you can find continued meaning in the holidays and in life. You can continue to live and love fully. You must grieve but you can also celebrate. This book will help you find ways that are right for you to do both.

Setting your intention to heal

It takes a true commitment to heal in your grief. Yes, you are changed, but with commitment and intention you can and will become whole again. Commitment goes hand in hand with the concept of "setting your intention." Intention is defined as being conscious of what you want to experience. A close cousin to "affirmation," it is using the power of positive thought to produce a desired result.

We often use the power of intention in our everyday lives. If you have an important presentation at work, you might focus your thoughts in the days before the presentation on speaking clearly and confidently. You might envision yourself being well-received by your colleagues. You have set your intention to succeed in this presentation. By contrast, if you focus on the many ways your presentation can fail, and you succumb to your anxiety, you are much less likely to give a good presentation.

How can you use this in your journey through holiday grief? By setting your intention to heal.

When you set your intention to heal, you make a true commitment to positively influence the course of your journey. You choose between being what I call a "passive witness" or an "active participant" in your grief. I'm sure you have heard this tired cliché: Time heals all wounds. Yet, time alone has nothing to do with healing. To heal, you must be willing to learn about the mystery of the grief journey. It can't be fixed or "resolved," it can only be soothed and "reconciled" through actively experiencing the multitude of thoughts and feelings involved.

The concept of intention-setting presupposes that your outer reality is a direct reflection of your inner thoughts and beliefs. If you can change or mold some of your thoughts and beliefs, then you can influence your reality. And in journaling and speaking (and praying!) your intentions, you help "set" them.

You might tell yourself, "I can and will reach out for support during the holidays. I will become filled with hope that I can and will survive this loss." Together with these words, you might form mental pictures of hugging and talking to your friends and seeing your happier self in the future.

Setting your intent to heal is not only a way of surviving your loss (although it is indeed that!), it is a way of actively guiding your grief. Of course, you will still have to honor and embrace your pain during this time. By honoring the presence of your pain, by understanding the appropriateness of your pain, you are committing to facing the pain. You are committing yourself to paying attention to your anguish in ways that allow you to begin to breathe life into your soul again. That, my friend, is a very good reason to give attention to your intention. The alternative would be to shut down in an effort to avoid and deny your pain, which is to die while you are still alive.

Turning to ritual

Setting your intention to mourn and heal during the holidays—and beyond—is one important way to move forward in your grief journey. Harnessing the power of ritual is another.

We create holiday rituals because everyday activities and normal conversation cannot capture our most profound thoughts and feelings. Rituals give them voice and shape. So, we decorate our Christmas trees, light our menorahs, give gifts, hold hands and say prayers. What words could we possibly utter that would capture so well our feelings at these moments?

During your time of grief, the very rituals of the holidays can help you survive them. Try participating in some of your normal holiday traditions but with a focus on your grief. When you light candles in your home, do it in honor of the person who died. When you sing holiday songs, allow yourself to embrace any grief feelings the music stirs within you. Attending services at your place of worship, praying and meditating are other meaningful ways to tap into the healing power of ritual this holiday season.

You might also create a special holiday ceremony or private ritual in memory of the person who died. (See Ideas 53 and 55.)

The holidays are ritualistic and ritual can help you survive (and heal) right now. Remember this when you are considering whether or not to participate in your next holiday tradition.

Living in the now

Return once more to the holiday memory I asked you to conjure up at the beginning of this Introduction. Recall again the sights, sounds, smells, tastes and feelings.

This memory is so special to you because you were so very present to the moment. You weren't rushing about, thinking about what needed to be done next. You weren't worried about work and bills and household chores. Instead, you were there, savoring the now.

When your grief overwhelms you this holiday season, try focusing on the now. Your grief wants you to live in the past through memories of the precious person who died. Remembering is indeed important, and your memories will always be a special part of your life.

Your grief will also project you into the future at times. You will worry about what the coming months and years hold for you. Looking ahead is also a normal and natural part of grief.

But when remembering and projecting exhaust you—and they will— return yourself to the present moment.

Concentrate on what is going on around you right now. Hear the sounds and see the sights. If you are in the company of a friend or beloved family member, be present to that person. Listen to her and notice the amazing reality of her being.

Try drawing on the power of now to find continued meaning in your holidays and in your life.

How to use this book

This book's intention is to help you blend mourning and celebration during the holidays in ways that work for you and your family. It contains 100 practical thoughts and ideas to help you understand your holiday grief and, even more important, to express it. Grief expressed is called mourning, and mourning helps you heal.

You'll notice that I have used the generic term "holiday season" throughout this book. By that I mostly mean the winter holidays book-ended, in the United States, by Thanksgiving and New Year's Day. In between are the spiritual/religious holidays of Christmas, Hanukkah and Kwanzaa. But whatever holidays you celebrate and no matter where you live, the principles in this book apply to the holidays that are most meaningful to you—including other holidays, birthdays and anniversaries sprinkled throughout the calendar year.

I invite you to flip this book open to any page. Read through the Idea you encounter and decide if it speaks to your unique holiday grief. If it doesn't, try another Idea. If it does, try the exercise described in the carpe diem (which means "seize the day"). The carpe diem exercises are there to help you do something with your grief, right here and now, empowering you to be an active participant in your own healing.

And if you are able to muster the courage to actively mourn, you will begin to heal. And you will grow. And you will live and love again.

I wish you peace this holiday season. God bless you. I hope we meet one day.

Alan D. Wolfelt

"In the depth of winter, I finally learned that there was in me an invincible summer."
— Albert Camus

1.
BE COMPASSIONATE
WITH YOURSELF

- Don't judge yourself or set your expectations too high. Be kind to yourself.

- The journey through grief is a long and difficult one. It is also a journey for which there is no preparation.

- Be compassionate with yourself as you encounter painful thoughts and feelings. Self-compassion in grief is essential year-round, but especially during the emotionally-fraught holidays.

- Let your holiday grief be what it is. And let yourself—your new, grieving self—be who you are.

CARPE DIEM
Give yourself a rest break today. Lay your body down for at least 20 minutes during the afternoon and relax your muscles. Sleep if sleep comes.

2.
SAVOR THE MOMENT

- When you think about the holiday season as this vast period of celebration from Thanksgiving to New Year's, it can definitely seem overwhelming, especially when you're in mourning.

- But when you take them one day at a time—or better yet, one moment at a time—the holidays have much to offer mourners:
  - Mourners need downtime to retreat into their grief. The holidays provide a lull in our normally hectic schedules.
  - Mourners need the presence and support of people who love them. The holidays give us opportunities to be with our friends and family.
  - Mourners need to remember the person who died. The holidays encourage memory-sharing.

- This holiday season, take what you need from the holidays— moment by moment—and discard the rest.

CARPE DIEM
Right now, turn off your mind and attend to the moment. Pay attention to what you are hearing, tasting, smelling, seeing, feeling on your skin. Savor the sensation of life.

3.
DON'T CATASTROPHIZE

- Don't assume that your holidays will be totally miserable this year.

- Yes, if you are actively mourning, you will experience pain and sadness. But if you spend time in the company of people you love, you may also experience moments of great joy and hope.

- Be open to the possibility of happiness during the holidays. And if and when you do feel glimpses of happiness, do so without guilt. You are still alive, and finding happiness means you are carrying on with your life's purpose.

CARPE DIEM
For a minute or two, allow yourself to think about what could turn out to be a miserable holiday experience. Now re-visualize that same experience, this time foreseeing moments of joy and happiness intermingled with your grief. Set your intention on the latter.

4.
SURVIVE

- Early grief is often characterized by feelings of shock and numbness. You may feel dazed or stunned.

- These normal feelings are nature's way of temporarily protecting you from the full reality of the death. They help insulate you psychologically until you are more able to tolerate what you don't want to believe.

- As disbelief wanes, pain waxes. Grief usually hurts more before it hurts less.

- If the death was very recent, you may be in survival mode this holiday season. If that's true for you, it's OK—the world will keep turning whether you participate in the holidays or not.

CARPE DIEM
Allow yourself to be in survival mode this holiday season if that's where you find yourself. Indulge your survival instincts. Do what they tell you to do and let the rest slide.

5.
KEEP WHAT MATTERS

- Because you're in mourning this year, you may feel like not "doing" the holidays at all. That's an understandable thought!

- But your family's holiday traditions are an important part of your shared history as well as your continuing lives. You may find yourself wanting to celebrate as you always have for memory's sake.

- You might also consider simplifying your holiday rituals instead of abandoning them altogether. Keep the traditions that matter most to you and set the others aside, at least for now.

- Simplify by keeping a tradition but paring it down. Instead of hosting a formal sit-down dinner, for example, have a buffet potluck or ask someone else to host the dinner. Use disposable plates instead of your good china.

CARPE DIEM
Make a list of all your holiday traditions and circle those that you think are most essential.

6.
FIND YOUR GRIEF'S FINGERPRINT

- Your grief is unique. It is the one-of-a-kind product of the unique relationship and love you shared with the person who died.

- Just as the lines and whorls of your fingerprint are like no one else's, your grief will be unlike anyone else's.

- While in many ways your thoughts and feelings will be similar to those of others who have experienced the death of someone loved, they will not be identical.

- Accept your unique thoughts and feelings this holiday season. Find ways to mourn that work for you. When others judge your grief, don't take it to heart.

CARPE DIEM
What is your grief telling you to do (or not do) this minute?
Honor its voice.

7.
ATTEND TO YOUR SPIRIT

- Above all, mourning is a spiritual journey of the heart and soul. And the holidays are a spiritual time of year. Together the two demand your spiritual time and attention.

- If you have faith or spirituality, express it in ways that seem appropriate to you.

- Attending church or your place of worship, reading religious texts, and praying are a few conventional ways of expressing your faith. Be open to less conventional ways, as well, such as meditating or spending time alone in nature.

CARPE DIEM
Where do you feel most spiritually connected to the person who died? Go there today and feel her presence.

8.
UNDERSTAND THE DIFFERENCE BETWEEN GRIEF AND MOURNING

- Grief is the constellation of internal thoughts and feelings we have when someone loved dies.

- Mourning is the outward expression of grief.

- Everyone grieves when someone loved dies, but if we are to heal, we must also mourn.

- Many of the ideas in this book are intended to help you find ways during the holiday season to mourn deaths that have impacted your life. If you express your grief outside of yourself, the holidays will be richer and perhaps less painful.

CARPE DIEM
How does your grief feel right now? Mourn your grief by telling someone you trust about your thoughts and feelings right now.

9.
UNDERSTAND THE SIX NEEDS OF MOURNING

Need #1: Acknowledge the reality of the death.

- You must gently confront the difficult reality that someone you love is dead and will never physically be present to you again.

- Whether the death was sudden or anticipated, acknowledging the full reality of the loss may occur over weeks and months.

- You will first acknowledge the reality of the loss with your head. Only over time will you come to acknowledge it with your heart.

- At times you may push away the reality of the death. This is normal. You will come to integrate the reality in doses as you are ready.

CARPE DIEM
Tell someone about the death today. Talking about it will help you work on this important need.

10.

UNDERSTAND THE SIX NEEDS
OF MOURNING

Need #2: Embrace the pain of the loss.

• This need requires mourners to embrace the pain of their loss—
something we naturally don't want to do. It is easier to avoid,
repress or push away the pain of grief than it is to confront it.

• It is in embracing your grief, however, that you will learn to reconcile yourself to it.

• During the holidays, your pain may be closer to the surface. The ritual and intimacy of the holidays may make you more emotional.
Remember that your emotions are normal and natural, and when
you feel them it means it's time for you to feel them.

• If you keep yourself too busy during the holidays, you may leave
yourself no time to work on this critical need of mourning. Don't
overschedule and don't try to "keep busy" simply to avoid the pain.

CARPE DIEM
If you feel up to it, allow yourself a time for embracing pain
today. Dedicate 15 minutes to thinking about and feeling the
loss. Reach out to someone who doesn't try to take your pain
away and spend some time with him.

11.

UNDERSTAND THE SIX NEEDS OF MOURNING

Need #3: Remember the person who died.

• When someone loved dies, they live on in us through memory. To heal, you need to actively remember the person who died and commemorate the life that was lived.

• Never let anyone take your memories away in a misguided attempt to save you from pain. "Try to stop thinking about her" is not good advice.

• A wonderful thing about the holidays is that they encourage us to remember those we love. Even though it may hurt to remember, don't forget that remembering the past makes hoping for the future possible.

CARPE DIEM

Think about the earliest memories of holidays spent with the person who died. Do you have photographs from those years? If so, get them out and spend some time cherishing them today.

12.

UNDERSTAND THE SIX NEEDS
OF MOURNING

Need #4: Develop a new self-identity.

• Part of your self-identity was formed by the relationship you had with the person who died.

• You may have gone from being a "wife" to a "widow" or from a "parent" to a "bereaved parent." The way you defined yourself and the way society defines you is changed.

• Even your holiday self has changed. You may have gone from loving the holidays to dreading them or from being a big holiday baker to not wanting to spend a minute in the kitchen. The holidays will be different this year in part because you're different this year.

• You need to re-anchor yourself, to reconstruct your self-identity. This is arduous and painful work.

• Many mourners discover that as they work on this need, they ultimately discover some positive changes, such as becoming more caring or less judgmental.

CARPE DIEM

Write out a response to this prompt:

I used to be _____. Now that _____ died,
I am _____. This makes me feel _____.

Keep writing as long as you want.

13.

UNDERSTAND THE SIX NEEDS OF MOURNING

Need #5: Search for meaning.

- When someone loved dies, we naturally question the meaning and purpose of life and death.

- "Why?" questions may surface uncontrollably and often precede "How" questions. "Why did this happen?" comes before "How will I go on living?"

- Part of your struggle with the holidays will likely involve trying to find ongoing meaning in them. It may seem like the holidays are meaningless this year. Trust that in time and through the work of mourning, you will find meaning in the holidays again.

- You will probably question your philosophy of life and explore religious and spiritual values as you work on this need. Remember that having faith or spirituality does not negate your need to mourn. "Blessed are those who mourn for they shall be comforted."

CARPE DIEM

Think about what the holidays mean to you and how that meaning may feel different this year. What can you do to restore meaning in the holidays?

14.
UNDERSTAND THE SIX NEEDS OF MOURNING

Need #6: Receive ongoing support from others.

• As mourners, we need the love and understanding of others if we are to heal. When your friends and family reach out to you during the holidays, accept their support. Let them spend time with you and take care of you. You need their help and they need to give it.

• Don't feel ashamed by your dependence on others right now. Instead, revel in the knowledge that others care about you.

• Unfortunately, our society places too much value on "carrying on" and "doing well" after a death. So, many mourners are abandoned by their friends and family soon after the death. If you find yourself alone this holiday season, reach out to neighbors, people at your place of worship, or a grief support group.

• Grief is a process, not an event, and you will need the continued support of your friends and family for weeks, months and years.

CARPE DIEM

Sometimes your friends want to support you but don't know how. Ask. Call your closest friend right now and ask her to help you through the holidays. Suggest specifically how she could most help.

15.
KNOW THAT GRIEF DOES NOT PROCEED IN ORDERLY, PREDICTABLE "STAGES"

- Though the "Needs of Mourning" are numbered 1-6, grief is not an orderly progression towards healing. Don't fall into the trap of thinking your grief journey will be predictable or always forward-moving.

- Mourners often tell me that they thought the holidays would be worse than they actually turned out to be. Grief can be unpredictable.

- This holiday season, you will probably experience a multitude of different emotions in a wave-like fashion. You will also likely encounter more than one need of mourning at the same time.

- Be compassionate with yourself as you experience your own unique grief journey.

CARPE DIEM
Has anyone told you that you are in this or that "stage" of grief? Ignore this usually well-intended advice. Don't allow yourself or anyone else to compartmentalize your grief.

16.

LET GO OF DESTRUCTIVE MISCONCEPTIONS ABOUT GRIEF AND MOURNING

- You have probably internalized many of our society's harmful misconceptions about grief and mourning.

- Here are some to let go of:

  - I need to be strong and carry on.
  - Tears are a sign of weakness.
  - I need to get over my grief.
  - During the holidays, I need to contain my sadness.
  - I must carry on holiday traditions just as I always have.

- Sometimes these misconceptions will cause you to feel guilty about or ashamed of your true thoughts and feelings.

- These misconceptions aren't true. You don't need to be strong—you need to embrace your pain. Tears are a sacred form of mourning. You don't get over your grief—you learn to live with it. And during the holidays, you need to express your feelings, happy and sad.

CARPE DIEM
Write a response to the following: I used to think grief would be _____. Now I know that grief is _____.

17.
MOVE TOWARD YOUR GRIEF, NOT AWAY FROM IT

- Our society teaches us that emotional pain is to be avoided, not embraced, yet it is only in moving toward our grief that we can be healed. The holidays may well help you move toward your grief, and that is a good thing.

- As Helen Keller once said, "The only way to the other side is through."

- Be careful if you find yourself thinking that you're "doing well" since the death. Sometimes "doing well" means you're avoiding your pain.

CARPE DIEM
Today, talk to someone else who loved the person who died. Share your thoughts and feelings with her openly and encourage her to do the same. Support each other in your grief.

18.
PREPARE TO ANSWER THE TOUGH QUESTIONS

• You may see many friends and family members over the holidays. Naturally, they will ask how you're doing. What will you say?

• "Oh, I'm doing OK" or "Not too bad" aren't really honest responses. You're probably not "fine," either.

• Be honest. Many of these people are looking for an opportunity to support you in your grief. If you're honest with them about your thoughts and feelings, they can express their caring and compassion.

• At times, sharing a detail of your recent experience is better than a general answer. Share something that happened today or something that's been on your mind this week.

• Sometimes people will be uncomfortable with your honesty, however. Our culture generally isn't very open about death and grief. When this happens, thank the person for asking and change the subject.

CARPE DIEM
Think about and prepare an honest response to the
"How are you?" question.

19.
COMMUNICATE YOUR WISHES

- The holidays are traditionally a time of joining together with the people in our lives. We celebrate our relationships at home, at work, in social circles. Each group to whom you belong may have its own separate celebration.

- Muster the strength and courage to tell the people in your life what your wishes are for the holidays. If you'd like their company but prefer to gather somewhere different than you usually do, say so. If you'd rather skip some of the celebrations this year, tell them. If you're feeling unsure about how to spend the holidays, tell them.

- I often say that people can cope with what they know, but they can't cope with what they don't know or haven't been told. Your friends and family want to help but may not be sure how they can. You can guide them by being direct.

- Be proactive in your communication. Make phone calls or send e-mails early on expressing your thoughts and feelings.

CARPE DIEM
Call or send an e-mail today to someone with whom you usually share the holidays. Tell her how you'd like to see the holiday plans unfold.

20.
GIVE THANKS

- The holidays are a time to take stock of our lives and give thanks for all that is good in them.

- Striving to have an attitude of gratitude will help you weather your grief.

- Don't misunderstand: I'm not saying that you should quit grieving and be happy. I'm saying that with effort, you can have both your grief and your gratitude at the same time.

- As you learn to reconcile your grief, you will come to understand that you can live and love fully again while still missing the person who died.

CARPE DIEM
Write a prayer or a statement of thanks for Thanksgiving
or another holiday. Plan to read it when you gather
with friends and family.

21.
PLAN OUT THE SPECIAL DAYS

- The holiday season may take six weeks or so, but there are just a few actual holidays. There's Thanksgiving Day and New Year's Day, and in between, depending on your spiritual and cultural heritage, there's Hanukkah, Christmas and Kwanzaa.

- Make plans for the days your family normally celebrates. Decide in advance where you will spend the day and how you will spend it.

- When you are grieving, "playing it by ear" on these special days usually only compounds feelings of despair and disorganization.

- Your plans don't need to be the same plans you always have. This year you might decide to do things differently. And don't forget to have a back-up plan in case you find yourself unable to follow through with your original plans.

- A caution: If you normally spend these holidays in the company of people you love, deciding to spend them alone may be a mistake. Remember—you need to accept the love and support of others if you are to heal. Some alone time is certainly necessary when you are grieving, but holiday solitude may only heighten depression and waylay hope.

CARPE DIEM
Get out your holiday calendar right now and jot
down plans for the important days.

22.

PLAN WHO WILL CARRY OUT THE HOLIDAY TASKS NORMALLY HANDLED BY THE PERSON WHO DIED

- For many families, the ritual of holidays means that certain tasks are usually completed by certain people. Mom may be the one who always wraps presents, for example, while Dad may always make breakfast Christmas morning.

- Which holiday tasks were normally handled by the person who died? If you make a list, you'll probably find that some are more essential tasks than others.

- Gather everyone together to talk about how your family will redistribute the essential holiday chores. Planning in advance will help everyone feel less frantic.

- Remember to ask for help. If you have small children, for instance, and feel it's important to put up a Christmas tree this year, ask someone to help you bring home and erect the tree.

CARPE DIEM

Right now, pick up pen and paper and make a list of holiday roles and tasks that used to be carried out by the person who died. Decide which tasks are essential and which can be set aside for now. Talk with your family about reassigning essential tasks to others.

23.
PLAN IN SOME ALONE TIME

- The holidays can be full of nonstop activity, but this year you need some downtime, too.

- As you schedule your days and weeks, block out generous periods of time for rest and renewal. Your grief will likely make you feel tired and you'll need extra rest.

- Your natural feelings of sadness will also need your undivided attention here and there. Without blocks of alone time, how will you think and feel through your grief? It may be tempting to pack your schedule so full that you don't have time for your grief, but avoiding it now will only make it worse later.

- During your alone time, take long walks, meditate, pray—do whatever helps you nurture yourself during this naturally difficult time.

CARPE DIEM
Take some alone time to mourn today.

24.
REACH OUT TO OTHERS FOR HELP

- Perhaps the most compassionate thing you can do for yourself at this difficult time is to reach out for help from others.

- Think of it this way: Grieving may be the hardest work you have ever done. And hard work is less burdensome when others lend a hand. Life's greatest challenges—getting through school, raising children, pursuing a career—are in many ways team efforts. So it should be with mourning.

- Sharing your pain with others won't make it disappear, but it will, over time, make it more bearable.

- Reaching out for help also connects you to other people and strengthens the bonds of love that make life seem worth living again.

CARPE DIEM

Call a close friend who may have distanced himself from you since the death and tell him how much you need him right now. Suggest specific ways he can help.

25.
HELP OTHERS

- Help others! But I'm the one who needs help right now, you may be thinking.

- It's true, you do deserve special compassion and attention right now. But often, people find healing in selflessness.

- When—and only when—you feel you are ready, consider volunteering at a nursing home, a homeless shelter, your neighborhood school. Over the holidays, you might find it rewarding to help with a short-term project, such as Toys for Tots.

- If you're well into your grief journey, you may find yourself ready and able to help other mourners by starting a support group or volunteering at a hospice.

CARPE DIEM
Do something nice for someone else today, maybe
someone who doesn't really deserve it.

26.
TURN TO YOUR FAMILY

- In today's mobile, disconnected society, many people have lost touch with the gift of family. Your friends may come and go, but family, as they say, is forever.

- If you're emotionally close to members of your family, you're probably already reaching out to them for support. Allow them to be there for you. Let them in. And remember that each grieving family member will cope with his grief in his unique way.

- If you're not emotionally close to your family, perhaps now is the time to open closed doors. Call a family member you haven't spoken to for a while. Hop in a car or on a plane and make a long overdue visit.

- Plan to spend time with your family this holiday season. Rekindle old traditions. Renew old relationships.

CARPE DIEM
Make holiday plans with your family today.

27.
FOCUS ON RELATIONSHIPS

- Instead of concentrating on everything you have to do during the holidays, concentrate on whom you are doing it for. Who do you care about and what would truly be meaningful to them?

- Focus on the people, not the production of it all.

- Of course, grief requires you to focus on yourself, as well. Each day, ask yourself: What do I need today? Be proactive in meeting your daily needs.

- Your relationship with the person who died still requires your attention; you must create a new relationship based on memory instead of physical presence. Focusing on this relationship means time and activities spent remembering.

CARPE DIEM
This year, instead of making a holiday gift list, make a holiday relationship list. Write down the names of the special people in your life and next to each name, write something you can do for or with that person that will strengthen your relationship.

28.
REMEMBER OTHERS WHO HAD
A SPECIAL RELATIONSHIP WITH
THE PERSON WHO DIED

- At times your appropriately inward focus will make you feel alone in your grief.

- Think about others who have been affected by this death: friends, lovers, teachers, neighbors.

- Is there someone outside of the accepted "circle of mourners" who may be struggling with this death? Perhaps you could call her and offer your condolences.

- If you're sending holiday cards, include special, individualized notes to everyone you can think of who is grieving this death. Writing the notes will help you mourn and reading the notes will help the recipients heal, too.

CARPE DIEM
Today, write and mail (or e-mail) a brief supportive note to someone else affected by the death.

29.
TELL THE STORY, OVER AND OVER AGAIN IF NECESSARY

- Acknowledging a death is a painful, ongoing task that we accomplish in doses, over time. A vital part of healing in grief is often "telling the story" over and over again.

- Telling the "story" means relating the circumstances surrounding the death, reviewing the relationship, describing aspects of the personality of the person who died, and sharing memories, good and bad.

- It's as if each time we tell the story, it becomes a little more real.

- Find people who are willing to listen to you tell your story, over and over again if necessary, without judgment. A grief support group is an excellent place to tell your story to others who understand.

CARPE DIEM
Tell the story to someone today in the form of a letter.
Perhaps you can write and send this letter to a friend who
lives far away.

30.
USE THE NAME OF THE PERSON WHO DIED

- When you're talking about the death or about your life in general, don't avoid using the name of the person who died. Using the name lets others know they can use it, too.

- Acknowledge the significance of the death by talking about the person who died: "I remember when David . . .", "I was thinking of Sarah today because . . ."

- Encourage your friends and family to use the name of the person who died, too. Mourners often love to hear that special name.

CARPE DIEM
Today, tell someone a holiday memory of the person who died. Use his name and relate as many details as you can remember.

31.
EXPECT A VARIETY OF FEELINGS

- Mourners don't just feel sad. We may feel numb, angry, guilty, afraid, confused, lonely or even relieved. Sometimes these feelings follow each other within a short period of time or they may occur simultaneously.

- As strange as some of these emotions may seem to you, they are normal and healthy. Allow yourself to feel whatever it is you are feeling without judging yourself.

- You may find yourself feeling guilty if now and then you experience joy during the holiday season. It's common for mourners to feel it's a betrayal of the person who died if they are not sad all the time.

- Experiencing moments of happiness and joy during the holidays does not mean you didn't deeply love the person who died. It merely means that you are alive and can continue to live.

CARPE DIEM
Take an inventory of your feelings today. Undoubtedly you feel sad, but what other emotions have you experienced in the last 24 hours? Have you felt anything that surprised you?

32.
TAKE GOOD CARE OF YOURSELF

- Good self-care is nurturing and necessary for mourners, yet it's something many of us completely overlook.

- Try very hard to eat well and get adequate rest. Eating too many sweets or rich foods over the holidays will make you feel even more lethargic.

- Exercise not only provides you with more energy, it can give you focused thinking time. Take a brisk 20-minute walk every day and breathe deep the winter air. (But don't over-exercise, because your body needs extra rest, as well.)

- Now more than ever, you need to allow time for you.

CARPE DIEM
Are you taking a multi-vitamin? If not, now is probably a good time to start.

33.
FOLLOW YOUR BODY

- Grief can feel very physical at times.

- Among the most common physical responses to loss are troubles with sleeping and low energy. You may also suffer from muscle aches and pains, shortness of breath, feelings of emptiness in your stomach, tightness in your throat or chest, or other problems.

- This holiday season, if you're tired, rest. If have muscle aches and pains, take a hot bath or an ibuprofen. If you're thirsty, drink water (and lots of it!).

- Follow your body's lead. It may be telling you it's stressed and you should listen.

CARPE DIEM
Right this very moment, what is your body telling you? Put down this book and meet its needs.

34.
DRINK LOTS OF WATER

- Grief sometimes overrides our thirst mechanism.

- Dehydration can compound normal grief feelings of fatigue and disorientation.

- Drink at least four-five glasses of water each day. Each morning, fill a 2-quart pitcher with water and place it in your refrigerator. Add lemon slices if you like. Make it a point to drink the entire pitcher by dinnertime.

- Try teas, sparkling water, juices. At holiday gatherings, avoid alcohol and caffeinated beverages.

CARPE DIEM
Right now, fill an 8-ounce glass with cold water and drink it without setting the glass down.

35.
SLEEP TIGHT

- Mourning is fatiguing work. Feelings of exhaustion and low energy are extremely common.

- Your body is telling you it needs rest, so indulge your fatigue. Schedule at least eight hours of slumber into your day. Develop a relaxing bedtime routine so you're ready for sleep.

- Buy yourself new bedding and a good new pillow.

- Lie down for short rest periods periodically throughout the day. Take an afternoon nap if you feel like it.

CARPE DIEM
Tonight, begin getting ready for bed right after dinner. Take your phone off the hook, bathe or shower, listen to soothing music, sip hot herbal tea in bed as you read a good book or favorite magazine.

36.
CONSIDER WHAT YOU LOVE
ABOUT THE HOLIDAYS

- After the death of someone loved, you are forced to reconsider who you are apart from the person who died.

- You are a wholly unique and separate individual, complete with your own hopes and dreams, likes and dislikes.

- Now is a good time to consider what it is you like about the holidays. Being honest with yourself about what pleases you may make the coming weeks more tolerable—even flecked with moments of joy.

CARPE DIEM
Make a list of the things you most and least enjoy during the holidays. Make time for the things you enjoy and abandon those you don't.

37.
GO SHOPPING

- Shopping involves getting dressed and going out into the world. Sometimes pushing yourself to do just this much will help you have a better day.

- Shop somewhere you usually don't. Browse through an antique shop or flea market. Visit an art gallery. Drive to the mall two towns over.

- Pile up your mail-order catalogs next to a comfy chair and spend all day lingering over each and every one.

- If you tend to buy things to fill some emotional need, don't go shopping. Instead, make a list of everything you've purchased in the last six months. Then consider how you feel about those purchases today.

CARPE DIEM
Buy yourself something that makes you feel good, even if it's frivolous. Spend less than $10 dollars.

38.
SIMPLIFY GIFT-GIVING

- This year, consider simplifying the process of shopping for and wrapping gifts. Shop online. Have your gifts wrapped at the gift-wrap counter at your local mall. Ask a friend to help you shop.

- Buy the same thing for everyone. Choose a favorite book, bottle of wine or gift card and give one to everyone on your list. Or consider planning a family trip together in lieu of gifts.

- Participate in community-based gift donations instead, such as Toys for Tots and Santa Cops.

- Ask yourself: Do I feel like giving presents or do I feel like I have to give presents? If the latter, tell your friends and family that you're not up to gift-giving this year and ask that they honor your feelings by not giving you gifts, either. With the possible exception of gifts to children, it's OK to skip gift-giving this year.

CARPE DIEM
Instead of giving gifts, look into donating money to a non-profit organization in honor of the people you love. Heifer International (heifer.org) is a good model of charitable gift giving, but there are many others.

39.
MAKE HANDMADE GIFTS IN MEMORY OF THE PERSON WHO DIED

- As we've said, expressing your grief outside of yourself—mourning—is important to your healing. One mourning method that's effective for many people is art-making.

- If you find arts and crafts therapeutic (even if you're not particularly good at it!), perhaps you could make Christmas gifts this year. In doing so, you'll be mourning and accomplishing something very practical at the same time.

- You could decorate frames and insert a photo of the person who died. You could make holiday ornaments with the name and birth and death dates of the person who died. You could knit, sculpt, paint, write, cook—whatever medium moves you.

- Using cloth from clothing that belonged to the person who died, make throw pillows, quilts or cuddly bears. These huggable keepsakes are a tangible link to the person who died.

CARPE DIEM
What do you want people to remember most about the person who died? Think of a simple way to make gifts that capture this essence and will be treasured for years to come.

40.
GIVE A GIFT IN THE NAME OF THE PERSON WHO DIED

- Start a meaningful new holiday tradition by giving a gift in the name of the person who died.

- What cause, event or activity was important to the person who died? Choose something that was near and dear to the person who died and support it with an annual gift at holiday time.

- Donate money to a chosen nonprofit or sponsor an annual event with your contribution. If the person who died was a teacher, give money to his school. If she enjoyed gardening, donate to a local landscaping project. You get the idea!

CARPE DIEM
Choose special keepsakes from the belongings of the person who died and wrap them as holiday presents to give to those who will find them meaningful.

41.

BUY A GIFT FOR THE PERSON WHO DIED AND GIVE IT TO SOMEONE WHO WILL APPRECIATE IT

- If you could have given the person who died a special gift this holiday season, what would it have been?

- Buy the gift in loving memory, wrap it nicely and present it to someone who will appreciate it.

- You might give the gift anonymously to a needy family or, accompanied by a note explaining the gift's significance, to someone you love.

CARPE DIEM
Shop today for this special gift.

42.
ASK FOR THE GIFT OF MEMORY

- Tell your friends and family that in lieu of gifts this holiday, you'd like them each to write down special memories of the person who died. These notes or letters will become mementos your family will treasure forever.

- What a true gift it is to add the unique memories of others to your own precious cache.

- Place the memory notes or letters in the holiday album (Idea 59) or memory display (Idea 61) you've created.

CARPE DIEM
Talk to your friends and family today about your
special holiday gift request.

43.
LAUGH

- Humor is one of the most healing gifts of humanity.

- Laughter restores hope and assists us in surviving the pain of grief.

- During the holidays, joy and laughter are perhaps the very essence of our celebrations. You may not feel like laughing much this holiday season, however, and that's OK.

- But if and when you do find yourself laughing, don't feel guilty. Your continued capacity for happiness is not a betrayal of the person who died. Rather, it is an early sign that you will learn how to live fully again while forever grieving the death of someone loved.

CARPE DIEM
Close your eyes and picture the precious smile of the person who died. Hear her laughter. Smile back.

44.
PRAY

- Studies have shown that prayer can actually help people heal.

- If you believe in a higher power, pray. Pray for the person who died. Pray for your questions about life and death to be answered. Pray for the strength to embrace your pain and to heal over time. Pray for others affected by this death.

- The holidays are a natural time to reconnect with your spirituality. Draw on the spiritual power of the holidays to help you pray or meditate.

- Saying grace at the dinner table is part of the holiday ritual for many families. This year, say a prayer for the person who died, instead.

- If prayer at the holiday table isn't your thing, read a poem or a short spiritual piece in memory of the person who died.

CARPE DIEM
Bow your head right now and say a silent prayer.
If you are out of practice, don't worry; just let your
thoughts flow naturally.

45.
LISTEN TO THE MUSIC

- Music can be very healing to mourners because it helps us access our feelings, both happy and sad. It seems to bypass our minds and speak straight to our souls. Music can soothe the spirit and nurture the heart.

- During the holidays, certain songs and melodies have the power to conjure up vivid memories you shared with the person who died.

- If the death was very recent, you may find it too painful to listen to certain music right now. Wait until you're ready.

- When you're ready to use music's power to transport you to another time and place—and to embrace your deepest feelings, spend some time listening to your favorite holiday tunes.

CARPE DIEM
Think about which holiday song most reminds you of the person who died. Buy it on a CD today.

46.
PAY SOMEONE TO CLEAN YOUR HOUSE

- Recently I received a flyer in the mail for a cleaning service that claimed, "Life's too short to clean your own house." I tend to agree!

- Mourners are often overwhelmed by the many tasks of daily living, and cleaning may feel particularly burdensome to you during the busy holidays.

- Here's a thought: Let cleaning worries go! The health inspector probably won't shut you down, at least not for another month or two.

CARPE DIEM
Call a maid service and schedule someone to come to your house for a few hours this week. Or ask a friend who wants to support you to help you clean this week.

47.

TAKE YOUR PHONE OFF THE HOOK

- In our hectic lives, the phone is both a can't-live-without-it convenience and an annoying interruption.

- Sometimes we use the phone when we should be talking face-to-face.

- Next time you have an urge to call a friend, drop by and visit him instead. Notice how much more intimate and healing it can be to converse in person.

CARPE DIEM

Take your phone off the hook tonight (or turn the ringer off).
Don't review your messages until tomorrow. If certain
people will be worried about you because you're not answer-
ing your phone, let them know that you're taking your phone
off the hook for one night.

48.
TAKE SOME TIME OFF WORK

- Typically, our society grants us three days "bereavement leave" and then expects us to return to work as if nothing happened.

- As you know, three days is a paltry allowance for grief. Talk to your supervisor about taking off some additional time around the holidays.

- Some companies will grant extended leaves of absence or sabbaticals in some situations.

- If you simply can't take off additional time, request that your work load be lightened for the next several months.

CARPE DIEM
Get our your calendar and see if you can find a block of holiday time—maybe a week— to take off work.

49.
TAKE A MINI-VACATION

- Don't have time to take time off? Plan several mini-vacations this holiday season instead.

- What creative ideas can you come up with to renew yourself? Here are a few ideas to get you started:
  - Schedule a massage with a professional massage therapist.
  - Hike through a forest or tree farm and cut your own Christmas tree.
  - Go for a drive with no particular destination in mind. Explore the countryside, slow down and observe what you see.
  - Treat yourself or your family to a night in a hotel or bed and breakfast.
  - Visit a museum or a zoo.
  - Schedule a hot air balloon ride.
  - Hang out at the bookstore for an afternoon and read to your heart's content.
  - Go to a movie theater in the afternoon.
  - Get together for lunch with a friend you haven't seen for a while.
  - Go for a long walk.
  - Stop in the park to watch children sled or play.

CARPE DIEM
Plan a mini-vacation for today.
Spend one hour doing something special.

50.
TAKE ON A PROJECT

- Early in your grief, you may lack the energy to accomplish even everyday tasks. This "lethargy of grief" is normal, and while you are in its power, your body is telling you it needs rest.

- Later, however, when you have more energy, you may find yourself not knowing what to do with the time on your hands. This holiday season, consider taking on a project.

- Many charitable organizations need help during the holidays. You could volunteer at your local food bank or homeless shelter, or you could gather food and gifts for a needy family.

- Helping others when you yourself need help may seem backwards, but you'll find that in helping others you are in fact helping yourself.

CARPE DIEM
Take on a holiday project that has meaning for you.

51.
FILL THE EMPTY CHAIR

- Many families despair at the thought of the now-empty holiday dinner table chair normally occupied by the person who died. The empty chair is too painfully blatant a reminder that the person is gone forever.

- One way to face the specter of the empty chair is to fill it with someone else. Maybe you could invite a friend or neighbor to your holiday dinner.

- Reach out to someone else touched by this death by asking him to share your holiday meal. Together you can acknowledge the person who is missing while at the same time finding solace in each other's company.

- You can fill the empty chair and still acknowledge the person who is missing. Place a single flower in a vase on the table in memory and honor of the person who died.

- Or, your family might decide that leaving the chair empty is the best way to honor your grief this holiday season.

CARPE DIEM
Frame small photos of the those who have died and use them as part of your holiday centerpiece.

52.
LIGHT A CANDLE

- Candles are a lovely part of the holidays in many homes. When lit, they symbolize warmth, life and hope.

- Choose a special candle in memory of the person who died. You might select a large candle that will last for several holiday seasons. Look for a scent and color that remind you of the person who died.

- Each night during the holidays, light this candle in memory of the person who died. You may choose to make this your own private ritual or part of your family's ritual. Be careful not to leave a burning candle unattended.

- As you light the candle each night, think about the reasons you loved this person so very much.

CARPE DIEM
Shop for a special memory candle today.

53.
ESTABLISH YOUR OWN
PRIVATE RITUAL

- The holidays are full of group rituals. Family dinners and gatherings, services at places of worship, decorating and cooking—all of these traditional rituals are celebrated in the company of others.

- But this holiday, you might find it healing to add your own personal, private ritual in memory of the person who died.

- You might bring flowers to the cemetery or scattering site, for example, and spend a few minutes in quiet connection. Or you could spend an afternoon doing something that was meaningful to the person who died.

- Your private holiday ritual can be something you will repeat for years to come. It can be an ongoing way for you to honor your unique relationship with the person who died and hold his memory near and dear.

CARPE DIEM
What private ritual might be a holiday grief touchstone
for you, this year and in years to come? Brainstorm
a list of possibilities.

54.
ATTEND A REMEMBRANCE CEREMONY

- Many hospitals, hospices and funeral homes host remembrance ceremonies during the holidays.

- These ceremonies are times to gather together with others who mourn and remember the lives and deaths of those we love.

- Remembrance ceremonies typically involve listening to readings and music, lighting candles, and, sometimes, prayer. After the ceremony, guests often have time to chat with one another and share their stories.

- The act of joining together in our grief and ritualizing our mourning can be very healing. Especially early in their grief, many families say it was the most important thing they did during the holidays.

CARPE DIEM
Call your local hospital, hospice or funeral home and find out if and when a remembrance ceremony will be held this year. Plan to attend.

55.
PLAN YOUR OWN CEREMONY

- When words are inadequate, turn to ceremony.

- Ceremony assists in reality, recall, support, expression, transcendence.

- Like the rituals of the holidays themselves, the ritual of ceremony gives shape to our most profound thoughts and feelings and helps us express them in meaningful ways.

- The ceremony might center on memories of the person who died, "meaning of life" thoughts and feelings or affirmation of faith.

CARPE DIEM

Hold a candle-lighting memory ceremony. Invite a small group of friends. Form a circle around a center candle, with each person holding their own small candle. Have each person light their memory candle and share a memory of the person who died. At the end, play a song or read a poem or prayer in memory of the person who died.

56.
CRY

- Tears are a natural cleansing and healing mechanism. It's OK to cry. In fact, it's good to cry when you feel like it. What's more, tears are a form of mourning. They are sacred!

- On the other hand, don't feel bad if you aren't crying a lot. Not everyone is a crier.

- You may find that those around you are uncomfortable with your tears. As a society, we're often not so good at witnessing others in pain. During the "happy holidays," tears can seem especially out of place.

- Explain to your friends and family that you need to cry right now— even if it is the holidays (or because it's the holidays!)— and that they can help by allowing you to.

- Because the holidays can be a very emotional time, you may find yourself crying at unexpected times or places. If you need to, excuse yourself and retreat to somewhere private.

CARPE DIEM
If you feel like it, have a good cry today. Find a safe place to embrace your pain and cry as long and as hard as you want to.

57.
REACH OUT AND TOUCH

- For many people, physical contact with another human being is healing. It has been recognized since ancient times as having transformative, healing powers.

- Have you hugged anyone lately? Held someone's hand? Put your arm around another human being?

- You probably know several people who enjoy hugging or physical touching. If you're comfortable with their touch, encourage it during the holidays. Their contact may help you survive a time that otherwise seems unsurvivable.

- Take advantage of the physical presence of friends and family during the holidays. Sit near them and feel their loving energy.

CARPE DIEM
Try hugging your close friends and family members today,
even if you usually don't. You just might like it!

58.

UNDERSTAND THE ROLE OF "LINKING OBJECTS"

• You may be comforted by physical objects associated with the person who died. It is not unusual for mourners to save clothing, jewelry, toys, locks of hair and other personal items.

• Such "linking objects" may help you remember the person who died and honor the life that was lived. Such objects may help you heal.

• Never think that being attached to these objects is morbid or wrong.

• Never hurry into disposing of the personal effects of the person who died. You may want to leave personal items untouched for months or sometimes years. This is OK as long as the objects offer comfort and don't inhibit healing.

CARPE DIEM

Find a holiday memento that belonged to or reminds you of the person who died. During the holidays, display it somewhere you'll see it everyday.

59.

ASSEMBLE A HOLIDAY SCRAPBOOK OR PHOTO ALBUM

- The holidays will never be the same without the person who died, it's true, but you can incorporate holiday memories of her into future holidays.

- Go through photos and holiday memorabilia and gather up everything that belonged to or reminds you of the person who died. Photos of him during the holidays are particularly nice.

- Place all the photos and trinkets in a special album. You might also write captions describing the circumstances of each item.

- When it's finished, display the album somewhere everyone can see it. One of your new traditions can be rediscovering the album each holiday season and reminiscing together.

CARPE DIEM

Do you have photos of the person who died that were taken at holiday gatherings? Look for them today and begin placing them in an album.

60.
HANG A SPECIAL STOCKING

- If your holiday traditions include hanging stockings, consider hanging a special stocking in memory of the person who died.

- Instead of gifts, encourage others to fill the stocking with notes containing special memories.

- When the other stockings are opened, have someone read the memory notes aloud for all to hear and enjoy. Save the notes to read again at future holidays.

- The special stocking could also be hung in memory of all those special people in your family's life who have died. In this case, the stocking could hold be filled with loving memories of many people.

CARPE DIEM
If you don't already have a special holiday stocking that would work for this idea, buy or order one today.

61.
MAKE A MEMORY DISPLAY

- As part of your holiday decorating this year, why not create a special display of photos and mementos of the person who died?

- Arrange the items on a table or fireplace mantel.

- The display will become a place for everyone to linger over their thoughts, feelings and memories.

- Ask others to contribute items to the display.

- Or, if you are celebrating Christmas, decorate your holiday tree with ornaments, keepsakes and photos of the person who died.

CARPE DIEM
Choose a spot for the memory display and begin
placing items there today.

62.
PUBLISH A VERSE IN YOUR LOCAL NEWSPAPER

• Sometimes friends or family of the person who died will publish a memorial poem in the newspaper as a way of honoring the death and bearing witness to their grief.

• Write your own poem or find one in a book at the library.

• Verses often appear on the anniversary of the death or the birthday of the person who died. They're also appropriate at holiday times.

• Such verses are often published in or near the obituaries or the classified section of the newspaper.

• Or, submit a poem to a support group newsletter or ask to have it read at a holiday remembrance ceremony.

CARPE DIEM
Call your local newspaper and ask for rates and suggestions on publishing a memorial verse.

63.
START A HOLIDAY JOURNAL

- If we could only slow them down, we'd find that the holidays are really a time of introspection—a time in which we think about what's truly important to us and what gives our lives meaning.

- Even if you've never been a journaler, now may be a good time to try. Pick up a pen and paper and see where your introspection takes you.

- Don't worry about the quality of your writing; just write down whatever's on your mind and in your heart.

- If you write several entries in your holiday journal each season, years from now you'll have a poignant record of your progress towards healing. Rereading your journal each year will help you see your forward movement in the journey through grief.

CARPE DIEM
Buy a suitable blank book today and write your first entry.
Try completing this sentence,
"As the holidays grow closer, I wish...."

64.
BE STILL

- Take time out from the holiday hustle and bustle for stillness.

- Literally, still your body and your mind. Find a comfortable spot to sit and don't move. Turn off all distractions.

- Concentrate on your breathing—in and out. As you breathe in, you breathe in good energy. As you breathe out, you breathe out bad energy.

- When your mind begins to wander, return it to the here and now.

CARPE DIEM
Lie down—on your couch or bed or even on the ground outside, relax your body, close your eyes and be. Just be.

65.
WATCH THE SUN RISE

- The sun is a powerful symbol of life and renewal.

- When was the last time you watched the sun rise? Do you remember being touched by its beauty and power?

- Plan an early morning breakfast or walk in a location where you can see the sun rise. Hike to the top of a hill. Have coffee next to a lake.

- Maybe you could make a sunrise ceremony one of your new holiday traditions.

CARPE DIEM
Invite a friend on an early morning drive. Choose a fitting destination for watching the sun rise. Pack a brunch of hot coffee, rolls, fresh fruit.

66.
STARGAZE

- I don't know about you, but whenever I take the time to gaze in wonder at the star-filled night sky, I feel at one with the universe. I also feel more deeply connected to people I love who have died.

- Do you believe in an afterlife? If so, what do you imagine it's like? If the person who died is there, what is she doing right now?

- The universe is such a vast and astounding place, maybe heaven does reside there. Consider the heavenly possibilities for you and your loved one.

CARPE DIEM
Tonight, if the sky is clear, take a walk after dark and stare up at the moon and stars. Make a wish.

67.

SCHEDULE SOMETHING THAT GIVES YOU PLEASURE EACH AND EVERY DAY

- Often mourners need something to look forward to, a reason to get out of bed today.

- It's hard to look forward to each day when you know you will be experiencing pain and sadness.

- To counterbalance your normal and necessary mourning, plan something you enjoy doing every day.

- Reading, baking, going for a walk, having lunch with a friend, playing computer games—whatever brings you enjoyment.

CARPE DIEM

What's on tap for today? Squeeze in something you enjoy, no matter how hectic your schedule.

68.
SAY NO

- Especially soon after the death, you may lack the energy as well as the desire to participate in activities you used to find pleasurable.

- It's OK to say no when you're asked to help with a project or attend a party.

- Write a note to the people who've invited you and explain your feelings. Be sure to thank them for the invitation.

- Realize that you can't keep saying no forever. During the holidays, saying yes to the gatherings and rituals most important to you means saying yes to a continued life. Say no, but also say yes sometimes.

CARPE DIEM
Say no to something today. Allow yourself not
to feel guilty about it.

69.
GIVE YOURSELF PERMISSION
TO SLIP AWAY

- You may be invited to attend a number of holiday gatherings. It seems like the entire month of December can fill up with work parties, school concerts, neighborhood cookie exchanges, etc.

- You might want to pare down your schedule, but don't say no to every invitation. These gatherings are a wonderful opportunity for you to reach out to others and be supported in your grief.

- If you think positively, you just might enjoy yourself. And if you talk to others about your grief and accept their hugs, you'll likely feel better afterwards.

- So say yes sometimes, but give yourself advance permission to leave early. It's OK to attend your friend's New Year's party, for instance, but slip away well before midnight.

CARPE DIEM
What's the next holiday event you'll be attending? If someone is going with you, arrange a silent signal that lets him know you're ready to leave.

70.
IGNORE HURTFUL ADVICE

- Sometimes well-intended but misinformed friends will hurt you unknowingly with their words.

- You may be told:
    - I know how you feel.
    - Get on with your life.
    - The holidays are a time to be happy.
    - Keep your chin up.
    - This is a blessing.
    - Think of all you have to be thankful for.
    - Now you have an angel in heaven.
    - Time heals all wounds.
    - He wouldn't want you to be sad.

- Don't take this advice to heart. Such clichés are often offered because people don't know what else to say. The problem is, phrases like these diminish your unique and significant loss.

CARPE DIEM
The next time someone gives you this type of advice, tell them honestly how you're feeling or give yourself permission to turn and walk away.

71.
WATCH FOR WARNING SIGNS

- Sometimes mourners fall back on self-destructive behaviors to get through the holidays.

- You may reason that everyone drinks or takes recreational drugs as part of their holiday partying, but try to be honest with yourself about drug or alcohol abuse. If you're in over your head, ask someone for help.

- Are you having suicidal thoughts and feelings? Are you isolating yourself too much? Talk to someone today.

CARPE DIEM
Acknowledging to ourselves that we have a problem may come too late. If someone suggests that you need help, listen. Consider yourself fortunate to be so well-loved and get help.

72.
REASSESS YOUR PRIORITIES

- Death has a way of making us rethink our lives and the meaningfulness of the ways we spend them.

- This holiday season, think about what gives your life meaning and what doesn't.

- Take steps to spend more of your time on the former and less on the latter.

- Now may be the time to reconfigure your life. Choose a satisfying new career. Go back to school. Begin volunteering. Move closer to your family.

CARPE DIEM
Make a list with two columns: What's important to me.
What's not. Brainstorm for at least 15 minutes.

73.
THINK YOUNG

- It is the nature of children to live for the moment and appreciate today. All of us would benefit from a little more childlike wonder.

- Do something childish—blow bubbles, go sledding, skip rope, make a snowman, visit a toy store, climb a tree.

- If kids aren't already a part of your life, make arrangements to spend some time with them. Volunteer at a local school. Take a friend's children to the park one afternoon. Attend a children's holiday music program or play.

CARPE DIEM
Buy a holiday gift for a child today just because—perhaps a child who is also grieving this death.

74.

START A NEW HOLIDAY TRADITION

- Your life has been irrevocably changed by the death of someone loved. Your holiday celebrations will be irrevocably changed, too.

- This holiday will be different without the loving presence of the person who died. Honor that difference by starting a new holiday tradition.

- What did the person who died love to do? If he loved to run, maybe your family can start a new tradition of going for a walk or a run together this holiday. If she loved movies, watch one of her favorites together.

- I certainly wouldn't recommend throwing out all your old holiday traditions and replacing them with all new ones. Traditions are so meaningful in part because they endure for generations, through good times and bad. But it's also necessary to adapt and change as your life changes.

CARPE DIEM
Talk to your friends and family and brainstorm ideas for a new holiday tradition that honors the person who died.

75.
HANG A SYMBOL IN
YOUR WINDOW

- During World Wars I and II, families hung blue stars in their front windows to let their communities know that a member of their household was fighting overseas. When a soldier died, the family replaced the blue star with a gold star.

- The tradition of placing stars in the window helped people to communicate their feelings of patriotism and sacrifice. When the gold star was hung, it was a way for families to say to their neighbors, "Someone we love has died in service to our country. We are in mourning and we need your support."

- As part of your holiday decorating this year, hang a symbol denoting your loved one's death. Gold stars are reserved for fallen soldiers, so unless the person who died was killed in combat, choose something else.

- Your symbol could be a holiday ornament that belonged to the person who died, a wreath decorated with mementos of the person's life, or a banner created and adorned with messages by your friends and family.

CARPE DIEM
Create and hang a symbol in your window. Explain the
symbol to guests who visit your house.

76.
BE A SECRET SANTA

- Giving to others usually makes us feel good. It's more blessed to give than to receive, the saying goes.

- You could probably use some "feeling good" this holiday season. Give yourself a dose of pleasure by giving to someone else.

- Shop for small gifts you can give anonymously throughout the holidays. Candy, books and fast food gift certificates are just a few ideas. Groceries or meals might be appropriate for those in need.

- Write notes to accompany the gifts. Tell the recipients how wonderful they are.

CARPE DIEM
Identify someone you could be a secret Santa for this holiday season. Give the first gift today, and plan to give at least three more this holiday season. Shhhhhh…remember, it's a secret.

77.
OBSERVE A MOMENT OF SILENCE

- At an appropriate time in your holiday celebrations, tell everyone that you'd like to observe a moment of silence in honor of the person who died.

- This simple but touching ritual gives each person an opportunity to reflect on his or her unique feelings and memories.

- After the period of silence, you could say a prayer or speak a few thoughts aloud. This might also be a good time for everyone to share a special memory of the person who died.

- Try observing a moment of silence before a meal, before you open presents, or at the stroke of midnight.

CARPE DIEM
Plan when your family will observe a moment of
silence this holiday season.

78.
WEAR BLACK

- In Victorian times, part of the ritual of mourning dictated that mourners should wear black for certain periods of time to publicly indicate their grief. Widows, for example, were expected to dress completely in black for a period of at least one year. After that, touches of gray, mauve, and purple could be added to the otherwise black attire.

- While the Victorian mourning dress codes were overly rigid (as well as demeaning to women), they did serve the noble purpose of displaying one's internal grief externally. That is, they were a form of mourning—and mourning, as we know, helps us heal.

- This holiday season, consider wearing black to gatherings. The color is still a subtle reminder to others that you are in mourning and need their love and support.

- If you don't like to dress in black, that's OK. Maybe you could wear a black armband or a black tie or scarf to symbolize your grief. Or wear an article of clothing that belonged to the person who died.

CARPE DIEM
Look through your closet for black clothing you could wear to holiday gatherings this year.

79.
WATCH OUT FOR
SECOND-YEAR GRIEF

- The first holiday season after the death of someone loved is extremely difficult because it is the first *without*. But often its pain is blunted by early grief shock and numbness.

- You may find that the second holiday season after the death of someone loved is actually more painful. By now you have acknowledged the reality of the death not only in your head, but in your heart. The protective early numbness has worn off and the ache deepens.

- If your grief feels worse the second holiday season, don't worry— you're not going crazy. What you are feeling is normal and natural. Rest assured, though, if you continue to do the necessary work of mourning, future holidays will likely get better and better year by year.

CARPE DIEM
No matter where you are in your grief journey and how you
are feeling at this point, accept what is.

80.
BEWARE OF SEASONAL
AFFECTIVE DISORDER

- Seasonal Affective Disorder (SAD) is a depressive mood disorder brought on by lack of natural light during the winter months. It is thought that more than 11 million people suffer from SAD and that women are affected four times as often as men.

- If you think you may suffer from SAD, you may have a particularly difficult time coping with holiday grief because the holidays, of course, coincide with the weeks of the least daylight.

- Light therapy has been found to be an effective treatment for SAD sufferers. In areas where the sun often shines during the day, spending 20 minutes outside each day may do the trick.

CARPE DIEM
Before you were grieving, were you depressed during the winter months? If so, you may want to see your doctor or mental health caregiver and ask about light therapy.

81.
HELP A CHILD WHO IS GRIEVING

- Our holiday celebrations focus so much on children because witnessing their innocence and wonder brings us such joy.

- If a child you care about is grieving this death, he needs your help this holiday season. Some of his innocence and wonder have been taken from him and he needs to mourn his losses, too.

- Be there for the child and listen to her when she wants to talk. Watch how she plays out her grief. Answer her questions honestly.

- Model for the child how it's possible to blend mourning and celebration. You can remember the person who died and mourn his absence while still finding joy in the holiday season.

CARPE DIEM
Make arrangements to spend time with a grieving
child doing something he likes to do.

82.
SING

- Music is such an important part of the holidays. Each faith tradition has its own holiday songs lovingly handed down from generation to generation. Then there are the popular holiday tunes we all know and love. (Who can resist singing along to *I'm Dreaming of a White Christmas?*)

- Sing your grief. Put on a holiday CD and sing at the top of your lungs.

- Attend services at your place of worship and join in the singing.

- It doesn't matter, of course, whether you're a good singer or not. It only matters that you make noise! As the old Sesame Street song says, "Don't worry that you're not good enough for anyone else to hear, just sing….sing a song!"

- While certain songs are likely to make you feel sad, know that experiencing and embracing your sadness helps you heal.

CARPE DIEM
Today when you're driving alone in your car,
pop in a holiday CD and sing!

83.
WELCOME PLEASURE
WHEREVER YOU FIND IT

- Grief is often accompanied by a loss of pleasure in things you usually find pleasurable. We psychologists call this *anhedonia*, and it's very common in grief.

- During the holidays, you may find that your normal traditions and celebrations don't seem fun or pleasurable this year. Even though you carry them out with the best of intentions, you may find yourself feeling empty and numb.

- If you are experiencing anhedonia this holiday season, look for pleasure outside your normal holiday routines. If going to the movies gives you pleasure, for example, go to the movies. If watching football gives you pleasure, watch football.

- Of course, finding pleasure in harmful activities is a definite don't. Turning to alcohol, drugs and other "false" sources of pleasure will only do you harm.

CARPE DIEM
Call a friend you always have fun with and
plan to do something together today.

84.
WRITE A HOLIDAY LETTER

- Whether or not you usually send holiday cards, plan to do so this year if you have the energy.

- Why? Because a holiday card can be a good way for you to reach out to your friends and family about your grief. It is also a way to notify others who may not have heard about the death.

- You might write a generic letter in which you explain how you're doing and what has happened in your life since the death. I'm not suggesting you go into painful detail in this type of letter; rather, you can briefly (but honestly) share your general thoughts and feelings.

- If you would like to take this opportunity to thank those who helped you at the time of the death and in the weeks after, write personalized notes and enclose them in a holiday card.

- If you'd like, include a photo of the person who died and a copy of the obituary.

CARPE DIEM
Sit down and try writing a short holiday letter today.

85.

PREPARE FAVORITE HOLIDAY FOODS OF THE PERSON WHO DIED •

- One of the reasons that the holidays hold so much power is that they are multi-sensory. We experience the holidays not only with our eyes, but with our ears, our noses, our taste buds.

- Special foods are an important part of holiday traditions. Chances are your family prepares many of the same dishes each holiday, and everyone looks forward to those unique smells and flavors.

- What were the favorite holiday foods of the person who died? Continuing to prepare and enjoy them as a family is a time-tested way of keeping memories alive. Yes, having those foods around may make everyone feel a little sad, but it's a healing sadness borne of love and the honoring of a special life.

- Cooking can be a wonderful way to bring your family together. Be sure to include the children in helping prepare holiday favorites.

CARPE DIEM
Who's the holiday cook in your family? Help him plan the menu, shop and prepare the food, being sure to include favorite holiday fare of the person who died.

86.
MAKE A TOAST

- When you gather with loved ones to share a meal at holiday time, remember the person who died with a special toast.

- Prepare a few words before the meal begins. Write them down if it helps you feel more comfortable.

- If you'd like, ask each person at the table to share a memory of the person who died or mention the one thing they miss most about the person who died.

- This toast can become a new part of your holiday tradition. Year after year it can be a way to keep special memories alive.

CARPE DIEM
Write down some thoughts for your toast, or ask another family member to prepare and deliver the toast.

87.
PLAN FOR OTHER HOLIDAYS AND ANNIVERSARIES, TOO

- Of course, when I talk about the "holiday season," I'm primarily talking about the time from Thanksgiving through New Year's Day. But the principles in this book apply to all the various holidays throughout the year.

- How your grief will feel on other holidays will depend upon the connection you felt to the person who died on those days.

- If Valentine's Day, for example, was a special day in your relationship with the person who died, you are likely to feel your grief more profoundly on that day. The same is true of birthdays and anniversaries, such as the anniversary of the death.

- Make plans in advance for holidays and anniversaries. Get together with others who loved the person who died or plan to spend the day remembering. Visit the cemetery or scattering site. Making plans ahead of time will help you weather the storm.

CARPE DIEM
What is the next holiday, anniversary, birthday or other special day that was meaningful to you and the person who died? Right now, sit down and plan the day from start to finish.

88.
IF YOU'RE ALONE, FIND
WAYS TO CONNECT

- After the death of a spouse, a child or a best friend, some people find themselves alone during the holidays.

- Grief is so hard. Grief alone can be unbearable.

- One of the six needs of mourning is to receive support from others. If you're alone this holiday season, you need to make an effort to connect with other human beings. Invite your neighbor to dinner. Volunteer at a homeless shelter or nursing home. Join a group at a place of worship.

- If you know someone who's alone this holiday season, reach out to him. Spend time with him on his terms as well as inviting him to your holiday gatherings.

CARPE DIEM
So that you won't be alone this holiday, make plans
that involve other people. Reach out and you'll find
that others reach back.

89.
MAKE AN APPOINTMENT
WITH A GRIEF COUNSELOR

- If you haven't yet spoken with a grief counselor, rabbi, priest or minister about your grief journey, now may be a good time.

- Seeing a counselor or spiritual advisor for just a session or two over the holidays may help you cope better and focus more on what is important to you this year and what is not.

- If one-on-one counseling doesn't feel right to you, try attending a grief support group.

- Remember—reaching out for help does not mean you are weak. On the contrary, it means you are strong enough to be proactive in your healing.

CARPE DIEM
Call and make an appointment today. Commit to one meeting only and decide after the first meeting whether it would be helpful to schedule more.

90.
DON'T BE CAUGHT OFF GUARD BY "GRIEFBURSTS"

- Sometimes sudden storms of sadness overwhelm mourners. These moments can seem to come out of nowhere and can be frightening and painful.

- Even long after the death, something as simple as a sound, a smell or a phrase can bring on a "griefburst." The holidays, especially, are chockfull of sounds and smells that can call forth the memory of the person who died—and bring on your grief.

- Allow yourself to experience griefbursts without shame or self-judgment, no matter where and when they occur. If you would feel more comfortable, retreat to somewhere private when these strong feelings surface.

CARPE DIEM
Create an action plan for your next griefburst. For example, you might plan to drop whatever you are doing and go for a walk or record thoughts in your journal.

91.
ALLOW FOR FEELINGS OF UNFINISHED BUSINESS

- Death often brings about feelings of unfinished business. Things we never did, things we didn't get to say, things we wish we hadn't.

- Allow yourself to think through and feel these "if onlys." You may never be able to fully resolve these issues, but if you permit yourself to mourn them, you will be become reconciled to them.

- Is there something you wanted to say to the person who died but never did? Write her a letter that openly expresses your thoughts and feelings.

CARPE DIEM
Perhaps the person who died left some task incomplete.
Finish it on his behalf.

92.
GET AWAY FROM IT ALL

- Sometimes it takes a change of scenery to reveal the texture of our lives.

- New people and places help us see our lives from a new vantage point and can assist us in our search for meaning.

- Often, getting away from it all means leaving civilization behind and retreating to nature. Spending time in the Rocky Mountains near my home helps center me. But getting away from it all can also mean temporarily abandoning your environment and spending time in one that's altogether different.

- Spending part of the holidays somewhere new this season may help you survive as well as gain some perspective. After her mother died a slow, painful death, a woman I know took her family to New York City for Christmas. For her, getting away—just this once, just for a few days—helped her survive.

CARPE DIEM
Plan a trip with someone you love.

93.
COUNT YOUR BLESSINGS

- You may not be feeling very good about your life right now. That's OK. There is, indeed, a time for every purpose under heaven.

- Still, you are blessed. Your life has purpose and meaning. It will just take you some time to think and feel this through for yourself.

- Think of all you have to be thankful for. This is not to deny the hurt, for the hurt needs to take precedence right now. But it may help to consider the things that make your life worth living, too.

CARPE DIEM
Write a note to a special someone telling him how blessed you feel to have him in your life.

94.
PLAN SOMETHING SPECIAL FOR AFTER THE HOLIDAYS

- Having something to look forward to is an age-old trick that seems to work in many situations.

- If you're worried about making it through the holidays this year, plan a reward for yourself in early or mid-January.

- Your reward could be something as elaborate as a big vacation or as simple as a manicure or massage at a day spa. What restores and renews you? That's what you're looking for.

CARPE DIEM
Get out your January calendar and make
plans for something special.

95.

AS THE NEW YEAR APPROACHES, MAKE A LIST OF GOALS

- While you should not set a particular time and course for your healing, it may help you to have made other life goals for the coming year.

- Make a list of short-term goals for the next three months. Perhaps some of the goals could have to do with mourning activities (for example, make a memory book).

- Also make a list of long-term goals for the next year. Be both realistic and compassionate with yourself as you consider what's feasible and feels good and what will only add too much stress to your life.

CARPE DIEM
Write a list of goals for this week. Your goals may be as simple as: Go to work every day. Buy a gift for John. Take a walk on Tuesday night.

96.
MAKE A NEW YEAR'S RESOLUTION TO SIMPLIFY YOUR LIFE

- Many of us today are taking stock of what's really important in our lives and trying to discard the rest.

- Mourners are often overwhelmed by all the tasks and commitments we have. If you can rid yourself of some of those extraneous burdens, you'll have more time for mourning and healing.

- What is it that is overburdening you right now? Have your name taken off junk mail lists, ignore your dirty house, stop attending any optional meetings you don't look forward to.

CARPE DIEM
Cancel your newspaper subscription(s) if you're depressed by what you read. Quit watching TV news for a while.

97.
UNDERSTAND THE CONCEPT OF "RECONCILIATION"

- Sometimes you'll hear about mourners "recovering" from grief. This term is damaging because it implies that grief is an illness that must be cured. It also connotes a return to the way things were before the death.

- Mourners don't recover from grief. We become "reconciled" to it. In other words, we learn to live with it and are forever changed by it.

- This does not mean a life of misery, however. Mourners often not only heal but grow through grief. Our lives can potentially be deeper and more meaningful after the death of someone loved.

- Reconciliation takes time. You may not become truly reconciled to your loss for several years and even then will have "griefbursts" (see Idea 90) forever.

- During the holidays, freeing yourself from the unrealistic expectation to "get over" your grief can help you find a mix of mourning and celebration that works for you.

CARPE DIEM
Visualize what grief reconciliation would look and feel like for you. Work to get there.

98.
FIND YOUR HOPE

- To feel sad over the holidays is one thing. Everyone who misses the presence of someone special experiences sadness. Feeling sad is normal and necessary. But to feel despair...that is another thing.

- Despair is the loss of hope. Despair is hopelessness.

- If you find yourself in despair this holiday season, fight to find your hope. Hope is an expectation of a good that is yet to be. Hope is a belief that healing can and will occur.

- You create hope in yourself by actively mourning the death and setting your intention to heal. You can also reach out to others for hope. Spend time in the company of people who affirm your need to mourn yet at the same time give you hope for healing.

CARPE DIEM
Make a list of things you still look forward to in your life.
Make a list of people who are alive whom you care about.
Make a list of everything that gives you joy.

99.
STRIVE TO GROW THROUGH GRIEF

- You may find that you are growing emotionally and spiritually as a result of your grief journey.

- Growth means a new inner balance with no end points. While you may do the work of mourning to recapture in part some sense of inner balance, it is a new inner balance.

- Growth means exploring our assumptions about life. Ultimately, exploring our assumptions about life after the death of someone loved can make those assumptions richer and more life-affirming.

- Growth means utilizing our potentials. The encounter of grief reawakens us to the importance of utilizing our potentials—our capacities to mourn our losses openly and without shame, to be interpersonally effective in our relationships with others, and to continue to discover fulfillment in life, living and loving.

CARPE DIEM
Consider the ways in which you may be
"growing through grief."

100.
BELIEVE IN A BETTER NEXT YEAR

- This holiday season may be difficult for you. As you now know, one of the basic truths of grief is that it does—it must—involve pain and sadness.

- But there will be better tomorrows. Over time, periods of grieving tends to soften in intensity and duration.

- Next holiday season, you will likely experience less sadness and more joy. While they will forevermore remain somewhat bittersweet for you, the holidays can once again become that "most wonderful time of the year."

- Believe in a better next year. Believe in your capacity to heal and grow through grief. Believe in the enduring holiday spirit of giving and love.

CARPE DIEM

Write a note to yourself about next year's holidays, seal it in an envelope and tuck it among your boxed-up holiday decorations. Write down your intention to experience love and joy.

A FINAL WORD

"When the night has been too lonely and the road has been too long,
and you think that love is only for the lucky and the strong,
just remember, in the winter, far beneath the winter snows,
lies the seed that, with the sun's love, in the spring becomes the rose."
— Bette Midler

The death of someone precious demands your attention, and that is as it should be. Remember—to have the special needs of grief is not selfish or self-indulgent. Actually, self-care during this special time of year fortifies you for the ongoing ebbs and flows of your grief journey, a journey that leaves you profoundly affected and deeply changed. Your spirit—your "life force"—turns inward and slows down as a natural form of self-protection during holiday times. You must give attention to your needs without apology.

Above all, self-nurturing is about self-acceptance. When you embrace the reality that self-care begins with yourself, you no longer think of those around you as being responsible for your well-being. Healthy self-care during the holiday season frees you to mourn in ways that help you gently, with no timetable, integrate life losses into the fabric of your being.

Ultimately, your self-compassion will also help you be receptive to the love and concern of others. Not all but some very caring people do realize that you have special needs during holiday times. Allowing yourself to feel this love will activate healing, and provide hope that you can and will renew your spirit.

The grief you feel during the holidays is a very wise teacher. Grief teaches you that living fully after someone you love dies starts, in part, by realizing and acknowledging that pain continues. Grief teaches you that feelings of sadness and loss are not enemies to be fought, but friends to be understood. Grief teaches you that loving and caring for others are your most important needs here on earth. Grief teaches you to simplify your life and let people know each and every day how much you love them. Grief teaches you to slow down, to enjoy the moment, to find hidden treasure everywhere. Grief teaches you to honor the need to openly mourn the loss of those you love deep in your soul.

As you continue to heed grief's teachings, you can look forward to the days to come when your grief won't seem so raw. Your painful feelings of loss will soften and slowly be overtaken by warm thoughts and memories of holiday times spent with those who have gone before you.

It is my deep desire that you have discovered hope and healing in these pages. I bid you peace.

THE MOURNER'S CODE

Ten Self-Compassionate Principles

Though you should reach out to others as you journey through grief, you should not feel obligated to accept the unhelpful responses you may receive from some people. You are the one who is grieving, and as such, you have certain "rights" no one should try to take away from you.

The following list is intended both to empower you to heal and to decide how others can and cannot help. This is not to discourage you from reaching out to others for help, but rather to assist you in distinguishing useful responses from hurtful ones.

1. You have the right to experience your own unique grief.
No one else will grieve in exactly the same way you do. So, when you turn to others for help, don't allow them to tell you what you should or should not be feeling.

2. You have the right to talk about your grief.
Talking about your grief will help you heal. Seek out others who will allow you to talk as much as you want, as often as you want, about your grief. If at times you don't feel like talking, you also have the right to be silent.

3. You have the right to feel a multitude of emotions.
Confusion, disorientation, fear, guilt and relief are just a few of the emotions you might feel as part of your grief journey. Others may try to tell you that feeling angry, for example, is wrong. Don't take these judgmental responses to heart. Instead, find listeners who will accept your feelings without condition.

4. You have the right to be tolerant of your physical and emotional limits.
Your feelings of loss and sadness will probably leave you feeling fatigued. Respect what your body and mind are telling you. Get daily rest. Eat balanced meals. And don't allow others to push you into doing things you don't feel ready to do.

5. You have the right to experience "griefbursts."

Sometimes, out of nowhere, a powerful surge of grief may overcome you. This can be frightening, but is normal and natural. Find someone who understands and will let you talk it out.

6. You have the right to make use of ritual.

The funeral ritual does more than acknowledge the death of someone loved. It helps provide you with the support of caring people. More importantly, the funeral is a way for you to mourn. If others tell you the funeral or other healing rituals such as these are silly or unnecessary, don't listen.

7. You have the right to embrace your spirituality.

If faith is a part of your life, express it in ways that seem appropriate to you. Allow yourself to be around people who understand and support your religious beliefs. If you feel angry at God, find someone to talk with who won't be critical of your feelings of hurt and abandonment.

8. You have the right to search for meaning.

You may find yourself asking, "Why did he or she die? Why this way? Why now?" Some of your questions may have answers, but some may not. And watch out for the clichéd responses some people may give you. Comments like, "It was God's will" or "Think of what you still have to be thankful for" are not helpful and you do not have to accept them.

9. You have the right to treasure your memories.

Memories are one of the best legacies that exist after the death of someone loved. You will always remember. Instead of ignoring your memories, find others with whom you can share them.

10. You have the right to move toward your grief and heal.

Reconciling your grief will not happen quickly. Remember, grief is a process, not an event. Be patient and tolerant with yourself and avoid people who are impatient and intolerant with you. Neither you nor those around you must forget that the death of someone loved changes your life forever.

SEND US YOUR IDEAS FOR
HEALING YOUR HOLIDAY GRIEF!

I'd love to hear your practical ideas for blending mourning and celebration during the holiday season. I may use them in other books
someday. Please jot down your idea and mail it to:

Dr. Alan Wolfelt
The Center for Loss and Life Transition
3735 Broken Bow Rd.
Fort Collins, CO 80526
wolfelt@centerforloss.com

I hope to hear from you!

My idea:

_____

_____

_____

_____

_____

_____

_____

_____

My name and mailing/email address:

_____

_____

_____

_____

ALSO BY ALAN WOLFELT

UNDERSTANDING YOUR GRIEF
TEN ESSENTIAL TOUCHSTONES FOR FINDING HOPE AND HEALING YOUR HEART

One of North America's leading grief educators, Dr. Alan Wolfelt has written many books about healing in grief. This new book is his most comprehensive, covering the most important lessons that mourners have taught him in his three decades of working with the bereaved.

In compassionate, everyday language, *Understanding Your Grief* explains the important difference between grief and mourning and explores the mourner's need to gently acknowledge the death and embrace the pain of the loss. This important book also reveals the many factors that make each person's grief unique and the myriad of normal thoughts and feelings the mourner might have. Alan's philosophy of finding "companions" in grief versus "treaters" is explored. Dr. Wolfelt also offers suggestions for good self-care.

Throughout, Dr. Wolfelt affirms the readers' rights to be compassionate with themselves, lean on others for help, and trust in their innate ability to heal.

ISBN 978-1-879651-35-7 • 176 pages • softcover • $14.95

Companion
P R E S S

All Dr. Wolfelt's publications can be ordered by mail from:
Companion Press
3735 Broken Bow Road • Fort Collins, CO 80526
(970) 226-6050 • Fax 1-800-922-6051
www.centerforloss.com

ALSO BY ALAN WOLFELT

THE UNDERSTANDING YOUR GRIEF JOURNAL

EXPLORING THE TEN ESSENTIAL TOUCHSTONES

Writing can be a very effective form of mourning, or expressing your grief outside yourself. And it is through mourning that you heal in grief.

The Understanding Your Grief Journal is a companion workbook to *Understanding Your Grief.* Designed to help mourners explore the many facets of their unique grief through journaling, this compassionate book interfaces with the ten essential touchstones. Throughout, journalers are asked specific questions about their own unique grief journeys as they relate to the touchstones and are provided with writing space for the many questions asked.

Purchased as a set together with *Understanding Your Grief,* this journal is a wonderful mourning tool and safe place for those in grief. It also makes an ideal grief support group workbook.

ISBN 978-1-879651-39-5 • 112 pages • softcover • $14.95
(plus additional shipping and handling)

Companion
PRESS

All Dr. Wolfelt's publications can be ordered by mail from:
Companion Press
3735 Broken Bow Road • Fort Collins, CO 80526
(970) 226-6050 • Fax 1-800-922-6051
www.centerforloss.com

ALSO BY ALAN WOLFELT

THE JOURNEY THROUGH GRIEF: REFLECTIONS ON HEALING
Second Edition

This revised, second edition of *The Journey Through Grief* takes Dr. Wolfelt's popular book of reflections and adds space for guided journaling, asking readers thoughtful questions about their unique mourning needs and providing room to write responses.

The Journey Through Grief is organized around the six needs that all mourners must yield to—indeed embrace—if they are to go on to find continued meaning in life and living. Following a short explanation of each mourning need is a series of brief, spiritual passages that, when read slowly and reflectively, help mourners work through their unique thoughts and feelings.

"The reflections in this book encourage you to think, yes, but to think with your heart and soul," writes Dr. Wolfelt. "They invite you to go to that spiritual place inside you and, transcending our mourning-avoiding society and even your own personal inhibitions about grief, enter deeply into the journey."

Now in softcover, this lovely book is more helpful (and affordable) than ever!

ISBN 978-1-879651-11-1 • 176 pages • softcover • $16.95
(plus additional shipping and handling)

Companion
PRESS

All Dr. Wolfelt's publications can be ordered by mail from:
Companion Press
3735 Broken Bow Road • Fort Collins, CO 80526
(970) 226-6050 • Fax 1-800-922-6051
www.centerforloss.com

ALSO BY ALAN WOLFELT

WHEN YOUR PET DIES
A GUIDE TO MOURNING, REMEMBERING AND HEALING

When your pet dies, you may struggle with your grief. You may feel overwhelmed at the depth of your sadness. This book affirms the pet owner's grief and helps you understand why your feelings are so strong. It also offers practical suggestions for mourning—expressing your grief outside of yourself—so that you can heal. Ideas for remembering and memorializing your pet are also included.

Dr. Wolfelt has been a dog lover and owner for a long time, suffering the loss of his Husky several years ago. Many have been asking Dr. Wolfelt to write a book about pet loss to add to his comprehensive list of publications about grief. Here it is—in his compassionate, practical, inimitable style.

ISBN 978-1-879651-36-4 • 96 pages • softcover • $9.95
(plus shipping and handling)

Companion
PRESS

All Dr. Wolfelt's publications can be ordered by mail from:
Companion Press
3735 Broken Bow Road • Fort Collins, CO 80526
(970) 226-6050 • Fax 1-800-922-6051
www.centerforloss.com